From Campus to Career

25 Tips for Your First Professional Year

Leilani M. Brown

From Campus To Career: 25 Tips For Your First Professional Year
© 2022 by Leilani M. Brown

ISBN-10: 0-578-37204-4
ISBN-13: 978-0-578-37204-4

Visit us on the web: LeilaniMBrown.com

Dedicated to my heartbeat,
still the most important.

Introduction

Whew! We certainly didn't see that coming.

So much has happened since I initially wrote *From Campus to Cubicle: 25 Tips For Your First Professional Year*, my first book offering career advice to recent graduates, young professionals, and many others. As we mark two years (and counting) of the global pandemic, the way we work, live, socialize and do almost everything in our lives has changed. And yet, while so many things have changed (from what the first day now looks like to how we gather with friends, family, and colleagues) some things remain the same (such as not knowing how to log in to the company's human resource portal!).

Over the last seven years, I have had the privilege to speak to thousands — yes, thousands — of early career professionals, learning about their initial experiences at work and how they have navigated their first years in the workplace. They shared their unique concerns, such as great uncertainty about future job prospects, the need to feel connected to an organization's purpose, and a desire for improved diversity, equity, and inclusion at work.

This edition reflects some of those conversations.

A quick note on "respectability" before we begin:

Before we jump in, I would like to clarify what this book is not about — this book was not written to encourage the "policing" of one's behavior or adhering to a manufactured standard of "respectability." As I point out in tip #22, be yourself.

No one is suggesting that you use these strategies to manage others' unacceptable behavior in the workplace. If you believe that you are experiencing discrimination, harassment, or underlying bias, you should escalate the issue to your leadership or human resources department.

But, in a world full of "no control" bias factors, we can control how we show up, contribute and deliver results.

And that is what this book is, in fact, about.

Fair enough? Let's get started.

The tips

1. Work hard and deliver results.

2. Learn the business.

3. Always be curious.

4. Develop your own personal brand.

5. Use social media wisely.

6. Maintain your integrity.

7. Dress for success.

8. Write well.

9. Admit what you don't know.

10. Pause.

11. It's not all about you.

12. When you fail, learn.

13. Pay yourself first.

14. Avoid gossip.

15. Own the mistakes.

16. Relationships matter.

17. Master communication.

18. Do not steal.

19. Don't be a jerk.

20. Work parties are still work.

21. Feedback is a gift.

22. Be yourself.

23. Hoot with the owls & soar with the eagles.

24. Upgrade your email.

25. Find the balance.

#1

Work hard and deliver results.

We will start with the most obvious tip because it is just so important: work hard and deliver results.

During the first few years of your career, your job is to learn as much as possible and make your boss' job easier. Quite simply, you are there to deliver. With enthusiasm. Without error... or excuses. And, on time.

So just do it.

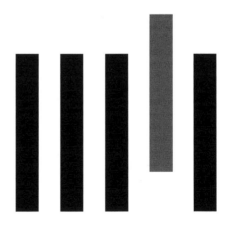

#2

Learn the business.

Pro Tip: Do online research to find recordings, panels, and podcasts of company and industry leaders speaking about trending and related topics.

Irrespective of your specific role — whether you work in the mailroom or frequent the boardroom — you should make a point of learning as much as you can about the company and the industry in which you work. The beginning of your career is the perfect time to ask questions, look for opportunities to join meetings, and volunteer for extra projects.

You should make every effort to understand your company fully, how it generates revenue and profit, and how your role contributes value to the organization.

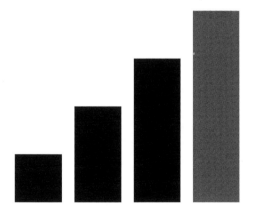

#3

Always be curious.

Pro Tip: Occasionally, read something with which you disagree, or watch a news broadcast from another country — an outside-in view can challenge or refine your thinking.

In addition to learning about your company and industry, you should cultivate curiosity regarding a variety of interests. Keep up with our dynamic and changing world.

- "Get" the news daily, including business, politics, sports, and even pop culture — all are potentially interesting in a "water cooler" discussion, chats with your colleagues, or may even be relevant to your role.

- Ask your boss or senior leaders what they read to keep current.

- Attend, watch, or participate in free learning events in your community, online or after-hours.

- Consider swapping out television programs with podcasts, TED Talks, or audio books.

#4

Develop your own personal brand.

Pro Tip: Avoid taking photos with cocktails. This is just a good thing to learn and practice early. Photos such as these can be taken out of context and may create an image you don't want to have to defend later. So, before you smile for the camera, put the glass down.

Your personal brand is, stated simply, your reputation. And, a positive one will serve you well over time.

Your work, your actions, and your relationships define your brand, so be thoughtful and deliberate about the same.

Be known for something — hopefully, something good.

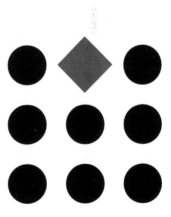

#5

Use social media wisely.

Use your personal social media as if the company is watching. Because it is.

Ok, maybe the company doesn't have 24-hour surveillance on your Instagram account, but what if you post photos of a wonderful night out with your friends at 3 AM but decide to call in sick under quarantine with the Coronavirus at 8 AM? Or, what if you decide to record a reel about how much you dislike one of your colleagues, and an online friend is her relative? Or, you tweet about how excited you are about project #TopSecret and sensitive information is leaked?

These posts can surface easily and have a very negative impact on your career.

#6

Maintain your integrity.

Integrity matters.

Having a set of personal values, and adhering to them — even in the most challenging of circumstances — is important.

Keep your promises and be honest.

#7

Dress for success.

Pro Tip: Buy good shoes and maintain them. In my experience, if your feet hurt, life will be unnecessarily harder. But, with the right shoes, you can feel like you are on solid ground, accomplish great things, or even feel a bit special. Once you make the investment, find a great shoemaker, and visit them often.

Pro Tip: If you work from home, dress your workspace for success, as well. If you can, find a place to focus that's free from distraction and noise. If you can't, headphones might be your best friend. Also, be sure your "office" is always camera-ready for both colleagues and external clients — use the background filter, if necessary.

You don't have to break the bank to be well-dressed and have a great personal appearance. And, believe it or not, you can even have a little bit of fun with fashion.

Rule 1: Read the cues of the organization. If everyone is wearing a suit, you should do the same. If the dress code is more casual, follow suit. When in doubt, ask.

Rule 2: Dress for the position you want.

Rule 3: Invest in good quality clothing and shoes (and wear them repeatedly — it's perfectly ok).

Rule 4: Maintain your items — it matters. Keep them clean, tailored, and polished.

Rule 5: Even when working from home — and maybe especially when working from home — get dressed!

You should find a look and style that is appropriate, authentic, and makes you feel good — that becomes your "signature" look.

#8

Write well.

Pro Tip: Enable the spell check function
on all your devices.

In the age of email, text messages, and Twitter, we have become very casual and sometimes lazy with our written communication. Writing well — without error, with precision, clearly and concisely — will differentiate you.

It also creates opportunities for the spotlight to shine on you. When a member of my team prepares something that is perfect and ready, I will forward it "as is" so that they can receive credit. If it's not ready, I can't share it... and I don't.

#9

Admit what you don't know.

Let me let you in on a secret: you were hired because of your potential. (Even executives are hired based on their potential.) Your first order of business is to learn. Ask questions now. There are no stupid questions... yet. But, a year from now, if you are asking what EBITDA means, or what unit handles M&A, or who the COO is, then... that's stupid.

#10

Pause.

Pro Tip: Create a "Pause" music playlist and consider using it while taking a walk to unwind.

If you are lucky enough to be in this world of work for enough time, someone will make you angry. Not something, but someone. So mad, in fact, that you are ready to give voice to the incredible sense of injustice you are feeling by telling them exactly what you think, that their mother dresses them funny, and that you don't believe that they are, in fact, qualified to be in the same room with you.

And, you might even be right. But those things, like many others, are best left unsaid. So, the real strength comes in your ability to PAUSE.

Wait 24 hours before you respond. You will likely find that your anger has subsided and you are able to give a far better response, if there is a need to respond at all. Because you cannot take it back.

#11

It's not all about you.

Things happen. Sometimes things happen to us. And sometimes we don't like these things. But when they do, I encourage you to take a step back and realize that there is a bigger picture. That the change you don't like, the acknowledgment you didn't get, the extra task at the last minute, was not likely directed at you.

Your boss didn't wake up with a master plan to ruin your day.

Get over it.

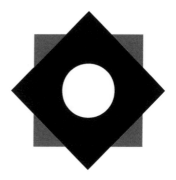

#12

When you fail, learn.

Pro Tip: Lean into the opportunity to have the conversation with your boss. Acknowledge the mistake, ask for feedback, direction, and insights on how you might do things differently in the future.

We all fail. If you are lucky, you will fail a lot early in your career, recover quickly and with little long-standing impact. But, when you fail or lose, don't lose the lesson. Don't miss the opportunity to ask yourself: What could I have done differently? How will I handle that next time?

#13

Pay yourself first.

Pro Tip: Learn the difference between your wants and needs. Live below your means to minimize and/or avoid debt

Pro Tip: Save for a "rainy day" — an emergency, unforeseen expense, a large purchase, or a potential job loss. From the first paycheck, consider an automatic withdrawal system with difficult accessibility to avoid using those funds.

Chances are you are eligible to participate in your organization's 401(k) or 403(b) plan and able to take advantage of the company match. ENROLL AND MAX IT OUT!

Why? You will establish early savings habits, you will benefit from compounding interest, you won't miss the cash from your paycheck, and you may be able to take full advantage of the "free" money granted by the company match.

Fine Print: This is not investment advice.

#14

Avoid gossip.

Ok, let's admit it — we all snicker at a little gossip now and then.

But, here is what I learned a long time ago: it's best to operate according to facts vs. hearsay, truth vs. innuendo, and official messages vs. speculation.

If you avoid gossip, and you are known to avoid it, you will rarely have to defend who said what. But if you engage in it, it's a slippery slope. You might find that the same people who bring you gossip about others are sharing gossip about you to others.

#15

Own the mistakes.

Pro Tip: Learn how to apologize.
Here is a quick formula:

1. Apologize.
2. Acknowledge the action and the impact.
3. Commit to correcting the behavior.
4. Apologize again.

We all make mistakes, have stumbles, or make errors. When this happens, and it is indeed your fault, it is important to be personally accountable for those errors. Don't place blame elsewhere — simply own it, correct it, and move on quickly.

Accountability will be important as you progress in your career.

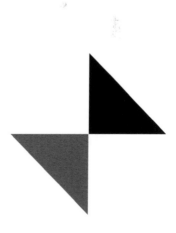

#16

Relationships matter.

Pro Tip: Send Thank You notes — handwritten if possible, and appropriate without being personally intrusive.

Yes, you will see these people again.

I have been working professionally for over 30 years. I am amazed by how many people remember me from my first years in the business. I am proud to say that many of them recall positive interactions. I have kept in touch with many of these contacts and have been able to call on them throughout my career and them on me. Their kids often call on me, as well. Develop meaningful and productive relationships throughout your professional career and you will not be sorry. It pays off long term.

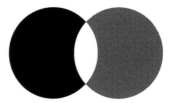

#17

Master communication.

Pro Tip: Watch your non-verbal communication. Remember that body language is also a powerful way to communicate. Be mindful of your posture, facial expressions, and even hand movements.

Pro Tip: Don't be afraid to make suggestions or offer an opinion when appropriate. Your thoughts and ideas are important, and offering them shows that you are engaged. And, you may give the team a different way to look at a problem, thus helping to create a better solution.

Everything we do sends a message, far beyond the very words that we say. When we communicate well, we make good impressions and can get things done. But, when we strike the wrong note, even unintentionally, poor communication can have negative and unintended consequences.

Working well with your colleagues requires learning the culture and the preferred methods of communication. For example, some might prefer email while others might prefer a telephone call or a scheduled meeting. It is better to ask versus guessing and manage to that standard.

In addition, and especially during a time of remote work and digital interactions, it is important to stay engaged and actually "show up." Turn the camera on and demonstrate that you are "tuned in."

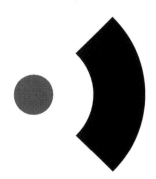

#18

Do not steal.

This may sound like one of the Ten Commandments, but, truly, let's talk about theft. Obviously, stealing money from the company is bad. But no one is going to hand you a checkbook to do that in your first week. However, let's consider other forms of stealing: abuse of time, falsifying your expense reports, taking office supplies, or spending a ridiculous amount of your workday on social media.

You can survive a long time getting away with these behaviors, but it sets up a lifetime of poor work habits.

#19

Don't be
a jerk.

Someone once shared an axiom that has stuck with me: "People do business with people they like."

I know that to be true. Being abrupt, abrasive, overly-opinionated, or rude to your colleagues — and everyone in your company is a colleague, from the mailroom to boardroom, because we are all in this together — will not serve you well. You will be avoided. You will not be granted the benefit of the doubt... ever. And, when you implode — and you will — no one will help you.

#20

Work parties are still work.

Soon, you are going to be invited to a "meeting" after hours. It will be held at a local restaurant or bar, your colleagues will be there, and food and beverages will be served. You might even hear music that entices a certain someone from accounting to break out the latest dance moves.

This "meeting" is called a work party, but is not to be confused with a regular party. You are still being observed, cultivating relationships with your colleagues, and you should still exhibit some level of decorum.

This doesn't mean you have to be a boring stick-in-the-mud — in fact, you should participate and enjoy the festivities. But resist the urge to get your fill of the open bar or dance on top of the tables. Remember... this is still a **work** function.

#21

Feedback is a gift.

Pro Tip: Consider proactively asking for feedback. Some questions you might ask your boss include: How am I doing? What feedback do you have for me? What should I do differently?

I once heard someone say this about feedback: "It might not feel good while it's working, but it's working for your good."

You should develop a strong feedback muscle early in your career, easily hearing what you need to hear versus what you want to hear. If you receive negative or challenging feedback, simply listen and demonstrate a willingness to learn and correct.

And, don't assume that if your boss hasn't shared feedback that things are going well. This is not always true. It might surprise you, but some bosses have a hard time giving feedback. Indeed, one of the worst things is for there to be an issue and for you to be unaware until the annual review.

#22

Be yourself.

Be your authentic self. Don't waste any time or energy trying to be anything other than who you are. When we operate and work from a place of authenticity, we are at our strongest. That is when we do our best work.

#23

Hoot with the owls & soar with the eagles.

Ah to be twenty-something again!

I remember the fun and late nights of beer, wine, and karaoke. But here is the contract you must make with yourself: if you are going to be up late hooting with the owls, then you had better be prepared to be up early and soaring with the eagles.

It's possible to enjoy yourself and keep your job!

#24

Upgrade your email.

Now that you have graduated, it's time to upgrade your email address. Select a clear simple one that closely resembles your name and is, hopefully, easy to remember.

Abandon prior email addresses that are overly cute, provocative, or controversial. In addition, it's a great time to move away from your school's domain address and consolidate to one account.

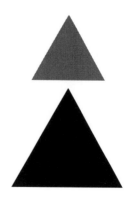

#25

Find the balance.

Pro Tip: When working from home, it is especially important to have a "start" and a "stop" to each day. At the end of each day and week, try to organize the next, identifying your priorities and creating a schedule for the days ahead to avoid getting overwhelmed.

Pro Tip: Proactively incorporate the five elements to a healthy and well-balanced life to manage stress:

1. Eat well.
2. Drink water.
3. Move your body.
4. Get good sleep.
5. Cultivate connection and community with family, friends and loved ones.

Especially now, as many of us are working from home, living from home, and doing it all from home, it is important to find a proper balance and maintain good health for our long-term well-being. Be as intentional about your health, wellness, and lifestyle as you are about your work.

Finally, be enthusiastic and have fun.

Go into this experience with an open mind, an open heart, and full of enthusiasm. Please accept my very best wishes. You've got this.

Congratulations and good luck.

To the dream team.

Cynthia Rose, whose edits, Oxford commas and em dashes always save me, and who did not allow me to thank her in the first edition but cannot avoid it now;

Yarde Noir, for hair, makeup, photos, and friendship in years past and for years to come;

Nehal Harley & Claudia Mark, for bringing the second edition to life, making the seemingly impossible, possible.

As well as... to my loving family, friends who are like family, and the many gracious colleagues with whom I have had the good fortune to work, for their kindness, encouragement, support, suggestions, and laughs while I finished this book.

Thank you!

Join us for a continued discussion
leilanimbrown.com

Connect with us on:
 @LeilaniMBrown
@LeilaniMBrown
LinkedIn.com/in/LeilaniMBrown

#FromCampusToCareer
#CuriousLeilani